IN FOCUS

GALAPAGOS ISLANDS

KINGFISHER
LONDON & NEW YORK

Copyright © Macmillan Publishers International Ltd 2018
Published in the United States by Kingfisher,
175 Fifth Ave., New York, NY 10010
Kingfisher is an imprint of Macmillan Children's Books, London
All rights reserved.

Distributed in the U.S. and Canada by Macmillan,
175 Fifth Ave., New York, NY 10010

Library of Congress Cataloging-in-Publication data has been applied for.

Series editor: Hayley Down
Designer: Jeni Child

ISBN (PB): 978-0-7534-7386-3
ISBN (HB): 978-0-7534-7385-6

Kingfisher books are available for special promotions
and premiums. For details contact: Special Markets
Department, Macmillan, 175 Fifth Ave.,
New York, NY 10010.

For more information, please visit
www.kingfisherbooks.com

Printed in China

9 8 7 6 5 4 3 2 1

1TR/0916/WKT/UG/128GSM

Picture credits
The Publisher would like to thank the following for permission to reproduce their material.
Top = t; Bottom = b; Middle = m; Left = l; Right = r
Front cover: Getty/ I love nature! - I love Brazil!; Back cover: iStock/ iStock; Cover flap: Shutterstock/ By FotoMonkey; Page 1 iStock/naes; 3 iStock/guenterguni;
4–5 iStock/4FR, 4t iStock/stevegeer, 4b iStock/javarman3; 5 Shutterstock/Michel Piccaya; 6 Alamy/Minden Pictures; 7t Nature Picture Library/Tui De Roy, 7m
iStock/4FR, 7b Alamy/imageBROKER; 8–9 iStock/4FR; 10 Getty/Gallo Images; 11t Getty/Visuals Unlimited Inc., 11m Getty/Visuals Unlimiged, 7b Getty/sodapix;
12–13 Nature Picture Library/Tui De Roy, 12m iStock/JAMPS, 13tl Getty/Mint Images, 13mr ALamy/blickwinkel; 14t iStock/2pter, 14bl iStock/marcelina982, 14br
iStock/stevegeer; 15t iStock/Rudemencial, 15bl Shutterstock/nouseforname, 15br iStock/NNehring; 16–17 Alamy/Michael Sparrow; 18 (1) Shutterstock/Fotos539;
19 (2) Getty, 19 (3) Getty/Andoni Canela, 19 (4) iStock/JAMPS, 19 (5) Nature Picture Library/Tui De Roy, 19 (6) Getty/Mary Plage, 19 (7) iStock/Dimitry Saparov, 19
(8) iStock/Bkamrath, 19 (9) iStock/stockcam, 19 (10) Alamy/incamerastock; 20–21 Getty/Steve Allen; 22–23 Alamy/robertharding, 22 Getty/MichaelMelford,
23 Alamy/GM Photo Images; 24–25 iStock/Uwe-Bergwitz; 26 (1) Shutterstock/Jim Cumming; 27 (2) iStock/hfrankWl, 27 (3) Getty/Tui De Roy, 27 (4) iStock.
waggers33, 27 (5) iStock/MortenElm, 27 (6) Alamy/Terry Wall, 27 (7) iStock/prasit_chansareekorn, 27 (8)iStock/mtilghma, 27 (9) iStock/MichaelStubblefield, 27
(10) iStock/RStokesPhoto; 28t iStock/RenHo, 28bl iStock/Arpad Benedek, 28br Getty; 29t iStockpiccaya, 29bl iStock/Rhys Mitchell, 29br Alamy/Nature Picture
Library; 30–31 iStock/pxhidalgo, 31t Alamy/Olga Kolos, 31b Shutterstock/Albert Loyo; 32t Alamy/Reinhard Dirscherl, 33b Alamy/imageBROKER; 34 (1) Alamy/
Minden Pictures, 35 (2) iStock/CampPhoto, 35 (3) Alamy/blickwinkel, 35 (4) Getty/Tui De Roy, 35 (5) iStock/WMarissen, 35 (6) Alamy/Amar and Isabelle Guillen –
Guillen Photo LLC, 35(7) iStock/burnsboxco, 35 (8) Alamy/Amar and Isabelle Guillen – Guillen Photo LLC, 35 (9) Shutterstock, 35 (10) Alamy/JeffRotman; 36–37
iStock/javarman3; 38t Shutterstock, 38bl Nature Picture Library/Pete Oxford, 38br Shutterstock/Uwe Bergwitz; 39t Nature Picture Library/Paul D Stewart, 39bl
Godfrey Merlen, 39br Getty/Andrew Peacock; 40–41 iStock iStock/MarcPo; 43–43 Alamy/Diane Johnson, 42b Getty/De Agostini Picture Library, 43b Getty/PETIT
Philippe; 44triStock/kalimf, 44 ml Shutterstock/Thomas Grau, 44br Alamy/Lebrecht Music and Arts Photo Library; 45t Creative Commons, 45m iStock/joecicak,
45b Creative Commons; 46 Alamy/Pictorial Press Ltd; 47t Getty/Wolfgang Kaehler, 47b Alamy Pictorial Press Ltd; 48–49 iStock/NNehring, 48m iStock/stockcam,
48b Getty/Mint Images, 49m Alamy/Arco Images GmbH, 49b Getty/stockcam; 50–51 Shutterstock/Michel Piccaya; 52 iStock/nok6716; 53t Alamy/Olga Kolos,
53m iStock/estivillml, 53b Shutterstock/Don Mammoser; 54–55 iStock/Tammy616; 56 (1) Shutterstock/Alberto Loyo; 57 (2) iStock/stockcam, 57 (3) Creative
Commons/Ratha Grimes, 57 (4) Shutterstock/Michel Piccaya, 57 (5) Alamy/Olga Kolos, 57 (6) iStock/miralex, 57 (7) Alamy/BSTAR PICTURES, 57 (8) Shutterstock/
Alberto Loyo, 57 (9) iStock/crisserberg, 57 (10) Alamy/Minden Pictures; 58—59 iStock/stockcam, 59b iStock/prasit chansarekorn; 60 Shutterstock/CapMarcel; 61
iStock/montgomerygilchrist; 62 iStock/estivillml; 63 iStock/Minden Pictures.

IN FOCUS

GALAPAGOS ISLANDS

BY CLIVE GIFFORD

KINGFISHER
NEW YORK

CONTENTS

A world of their own   6

TOUR THE ISLANDS   8

Meeting points   10

Violent volcanoes   12

In the zone   14

Close up: Getting prickly   16

Top 10: Islands   18

WONDERLAND OF WILDLIFE   20

Only on the islands   22

Close up: Crab-tastic!   24

Top 10: Island birds   26

Meet marine iguanas   28

Giant tortoises   30

Underwater life   32

Top 10: Unusual inhabitants — 34

Close-Up: Blue-footed boobies — 36

Island hunters — 38

ISLAND LIFE — 40

Ship ahoy! — 42

Pirates! — 44

Darwin's voyage of discovery — 46

Living on the islands — 48

Close up: Galápagos Day — 50

Living with nature — 52

Close up: Whale shark conservation — 54

Top 10: Landmarks — 56

All about conservation — 58

The great Galápagos quiz — 60

Glossary — 62

Index — 64

A WORLD OF THEIR OWN

Welcome to an incredible and unique island world. The Galápagos Islands make up an **archipelago**, meaning a chain of islands, in the Pacific Ocean. Their nearest major neighbor is the South American country Ecuador, which claims the islands as part of its territory. Ecuador's coast is over 559 mi (900 km) away.

Isolated from other lands and with no humans settling on the islands for thousands of years, the Galápagos have developed differently from other places. Unique and extraordinary plants and animals have flourished on the islands, astounding scientists, thrilling visitors, and making the islands world-famous.

Galápagos giant tortoises

INSIDE YOU'LL FIND . . .

... volcanic landscapes

DISCOVER the Galápagos Islands, from their violent volcanoes and beautiful lagoons to their scenic shorelines and varying climate zones, where different types of plant and animal life thrive.

ISLAND FACT

... wonderful wildlife

ISLAND FACT

ENCOUNTER the extraordinary wildlife that lives here, including many species found nowhere else in the world, such as brilliantly colored birds, giant tortoises, and sensational sea lions.

... people and pirates!

ISLAND FACT

LEARN about the people who explored and settled on the Galápagos, how they live and what impact they have on the islands.

TOUR THE ISLANDS

MEETING POINTS

There are 19 islands and over 100 **islets** in the Galápagos. They are all found at a junction in the Pacific Ocean where three **tectonic plates** meet and four different ocean currents flow into each other.

ISLAND FACT

The Galápagos Islands sit on the **EQUATOR**—the imaginary line around the center of Earth. It divides the planet into northern and southern hemispheres. The Equator runs through the northern part of Isabela Island, with Pinta, Marchena, and Genovesa islands north of the Equator and other islands, such as Santa Cruz, to the south.

The Galápagos Islands

Pinta

Genovesa

Marchena

Equator

Isabela

San Salvador

Bartolomé

Bainbridge

Baltra Island

Rábida

Fernandina

Santa Cruz

San Cristóbal

Pinzon

Puerto Isidro Ayora

Santa Fé

Puerto Villamil

Puerto Baquerizo Moreno

Floreana

Española

hot spot

ISLAND FACT

The islands lie close to a place where tectonic plates meet. Extremely hot molten rock within the Earth, called **magma**, can break through the crust to form a **HOT SPOT** of volcanic activity.

current events

ISLAND FACT

An **OCEAN CURRENT** is a continuous major flow of water. It is created by winds, tides, and differences in water temperature. Four different ocean currents meet at the Galápagos: the Equatorial, Cromwell, Humboldt, and Panama currents.

climate conditions

ISLAND FACT

The meeting of cold and warm ocean currents, as well as different winds, means that the Galápagos experience a milder and cooler **CLIMATE** than many other places on the Equator. January to April is the rainy season. June to December is the dry season, known as *garúa*.

VIOLENT VOLCANOES

Get answers to your questions about the volcanoes on the Galápagos and the features they produce!

How did volcanoes form the islands?

The Galápagos were formed by volcanoes on the Pacific Ocean floor. When an underwater volcano erupts, **lava** and hot gases from deep within planet Earth travel out through the crust. The lava cools and hardens in the cold seawater. Over time, many eruptions cause layers of rock to build up from the ocean floor until their peaks rise above the sea, forming islands, such as the Galápagos.

Lava flowing from Chico volcano on Isabela Island—cool!

What do eruptions leave behind?

When it cools, some lava forms patterns, such as Cueva del Cascajo—a lava tube that is almost 2 mi (3010 m) long on Santa Cruz. It was formed when thin lava flowed down a slope and the outside cooled faster than the inside, which continued to flow and left a hollow space behind.

What is a caldera?

A caldera is a volcano that collapses into itself to form a large, roughly circular crater. There are a number of calderas in the Galápagos. The biggest is Sierra Negra on Isabela Island. It is 4.5 mi (7200 m) by 5.75 mi (9300 m) wide. Enormous!

Are any Galápagos volcanoes still active?

Volcanoes can be active (able to erupt), extinct (won't erupt again), or dormant (haven't erupted for a long time but still could). There are a number of active volcanoes in the Galápagos. In 2015, Wolf Volcano erupted on Isabela Island. It spewed out red-hot lava and a massive column of smoke and ash.

COASTAL ZONE

The coastal zone is where the land meets the sea. A range of plants grows here, including a creeping vine called beach morning glory and low-growing *sesuvium*, which provides a carpet of color, turning green in the rainy season and pink and red in the dry season. Many species of mangrove trees grow along the coast and provide **breeding** and nesting places for frigate birds and pelicans, among other bird life.

mangrove
trees

HUMID ZONE

Higher areas of some of the larger islands receive plenty of rainfall to form a humid zone, allowing forests of scalesia trees to grow up to 65 ft (20 m) tall. Ferns, orchids, and mosses grow on or around these trees, providing homes and shelter for many different species, including finches, the Galápagos dove, and the Galápagos giant tortoise.

scalesia trees

Scientists divide up the different landscapes and climates of the Galápagos into zones: The coastal, humid, and arid zones. Each zone features different plants and habitats for creatures.

ARID ZONE

Occupying much of the islands' land, the arid zone is made up of dry and often rocky ground. Despite the tough conditions, some plants do flourish here, including acacia and palo santo trees, prickly pears, and other cactuses. These, in turn, help provide food, moisture, and shade for animals, such as land iguanas, rice rats, and lava lizards, which all live in this zone.

UNIQUE BLOOMS

The unique islands are home to over 600 native plants, many not found anywhere else in the world. These include the arid zone's lava cactus, which grows in spiny clumps up to 23 in (60 cm) tall and starts off as a yellow plant before aging to a gray color. Its flowers bloom for just a handful of hours each year.

lava cactuses

acacia tree

CLOSE UP

GETTING PRICKLY

Look, but don't touch! These strange plants are prickly pears. They are perfectly named as their fleshy leaves, which grow up to almost 5 in (12 cm) long, are covered in lots of super-sharp stiff hairs (or spines). Some types of prickly pear are found only on the Galápagos Islands. The plants produce tiny seeds, which are just 0.1/8 in (3 mm) long, but boy, do they grow! Mature plants reach up to 43 ft (13 m) tall, with thick stems more like tree trunks. Some prickly pear plants are 150 years old.

Food for thought

Different creatures feast on the prickly pear.
Cactus finches, for example, drink the sticky nectar
found in the plant's yellow-colored flowers. Ground
finches peck at the plant's fruits and
seeds. Tortoises and land iguanas
(pictured) get much of their
water from eating the
thick, juicy leaves.

ISLANDS

Which one is top when it comes to the islands of the Galápagos?

1 Santa Cruz Cracks

The most populous island, Santa Cruz features the Cracks, which are steep, narrow **canyons** with sheer drops. Formed when lava cooled, they're popular with hikers and swimmers.

2. Santiago Island's Toilet

A lava formation called Darwin's Toilet has a pool that empties and refills with the tides, just like a toilet!

7. San Cristóbal waters

On San Cristóbal, you'll find the Galápagos' only major **freshwater** lake, El Junco.

3. Isabela Island peaks

Isabela Island contains the Galápagos' highest point, Wolf Volcano, which stands 1609 mi (1.6 km) tall.

8. Rábida Island sands

Rábida island was formed partly by lava rich in iron, which gives its beaches a dark-red color.

4. Fiery Fernandina Island

La Cumbre volcano, on Fernandina Island, has a deep crater at the top that's 4 mi (6.5 km) wide.

9. Bartolomé Island steps

Bartolomé Island has a 375-step staircase, which you can climb to reach the island's peak.

5. Bainbridge Rocks

These islets lie off the coast of Santiago Island. One is made up of a worn-away volcanic crater with a turquoise lake that attracts flocks of flamingos.

10. Española Island caves

Around four million years old, Española has ocean caves and sandy bays, home to marine iguanas.

6. Floreana Island treasures

Around 100 people live on this island. It features the Devil's Crown—a ring of rocky spikes with a shark-infested **coral** reef inside.

Which island is your number one?

WONDERLAND
OF WILDLIFE

ONLY ON THE ISLANDS

The Galápagos are home to unique species of plants and animals, called **endemic species**. The ancestors of the islands' wildlife arrived there in a variety of ways . . .

LONESOME GEORGE was discovered on Pinta Island in 1971. He proved to be the last surviving Pinta Island tortoise. When he died in 2012, at the age of about 102, the species became extinct.

PLANT SEEDS would have been carried to the islands by the wind, the sea, or even inside birds—landing on the islands inside their poop!

ANCESTORS of today's Galápagos wildlife may have been carried there by the ocean currents. Shelled animals, such as tortoises, may have arrived by floating on their own shells; others may have floated on pieces of wood, using the wood like rafts.

There are around 40,000 Galápagos **FuR SEALS** forming large colonies around the rocky shorelines. These colonies are noisy; the seals make loud barking sounds to communicate with each other.

The **LARGE PAINTED LOCuST**, with parts colored orange and lime green, is found on almost all the islands in the Galápagos and nowhere else. It grows up to 3 in (8 cm) long and forms an important part of the diet of both lava lizards and Galápagos hawks.

GALAPAGOS SEA LIONS are one of the islands' biggest endemic species. They grow up to 8 ft (2.5 m) long and, at up to 55 lb (250 kg), weigh more than three adult men. They eat mostly sardines.

FLIGHTLESS CORMORANTS cannot fly and have short, stubby wings. These large birds are agile swimmers, though, and use their long neck and bill to lunge and spear octopuses, fish, and eels.

CRAB-TASTIC!

The Sally lightfoot crab is one of the Galápagos' most colorful creatures. Its 2–3-in (7–8-cm) shell and legs are a riot of red and other colors. The crab is named after a famous Caribbean dancer because of how quick and nimble it is. It can run forward, backward, or from side to side, jump from rock to rock, and even clamber up vertical ledges or cliff faces. Its speed makes it hard for predators to catch.

Not picky

These crabs mostly eat algae found along the shoreline, but they will try almost anything, from scavenging parts of dead creatures to catching other, smaller crabs. They even nibble on ticks picked from marine iguanas.

ISLAND BIRDS

Feast your eyes on this fabulous list of feathered friends that visit the Galápagos or make it their home.

1 Brown pelican

These 4-ft- (1.3-m-) tall birds use their big bill and the pouch that hangs below it as a strainer. They gulp in many gallons of seawater containing fish, then let the water drain out of their bill so they can swallow the fish whole.

2 Galápagos dove

If a predator threatens their young, dove parents will walk away from the nest, faking injury, to lure the attacker away.

3 Mangrove finch

Found only on Isabela Island, these finches eat grubs and insects. With only around 100 left, they are one of the world's rarest bird species.

4 Galápagos hawk

There are only around 300 Galápagos hawks left. They eat lizards, rats, and giant centipedes.

5 Red-footed booby

These all-terrain birds travel 62 mi (100 km) in a single flight and dive into the sea to catch fish.

6 Lava heron

These endemic wading birds are camouflaged by their gray color, but during the breeding season, the male herons' legs turn orange.

7 Waved albatross

These long-distance fliers travel to the Galápagos to breed. The female lays just one egg, which can take two months to hatch.

8 Galápagos penguin

Think of penguins and you think of ice and the poles, but this species makes its home right on the Equator.

9 Brown noddy

These sea birds nod to each other during courtship. They often perch on the heads of brown pelicans, hoping to steal fish.

10 Red-billed tropicbird

These birds boast incredibly long tail feathers: around 17 in (45 cm) long—about half of their overall length.

Which feathered friend is your number one?

MEET MARINE

BIG BEASTS

The marine iguana is endemic to the Galápagos Islands and varies greatly in size, depending on which island it lives. Iguanas on Genovesa Island weigh 2–4 lb (1–2 kg), while those on other islands tend to be heavier. The largest are found on Isabela Island. Some measure more than 3 ft (1 m) in length and weigh 28 lb (13 kg)—about the same weight as three well-fed pet cats.

heavy beast!

WHITE WIGS

Marine iguanas are mostly dark gray, but males change color during the breeding season with blotches of red and green on their body. To complete the look, many marine iguanas seem to wear a crusty white wig, formed by salt from the sea sneezed out by the iguanas and landing on their head. Famous **naturalist** Charles Darwin described them as "hideous-looking"—a little harsh!

male iguanas

IGUANAS

Say a big hello to the world's only sea-swimming lizard, the incredible marine iguana.

LOVE THE SUN

Marine iguanas are **cold-blooded** creatures, so they need to warm up by basking in the sun for hours each morning. When they swim in the cold ocean waters, their heart rate slows to half its normal rate to help the creatures save energy.

sunbathing

SWIM FOR SNACKS

Marine iguanas are **vegetarians** and live off algae. Iguanas swim for their food, swishing their powerful tail back and forth to move through the water. Their strong claws grip rocks while they use their teeth to scrape off algae. Male marine iguanas can stay underwater for an hour or longer and dive down to 32 ft (10 m) below the surface.

swimming iguana

GIANT TORTOISES

Answer your questions about the islands' most famous creature—the Galápagos giant tortoise.

Are they really giant?

They are the biggest tortoises in the world. Adults are about 4 ft (1.2 m) long, 20 in (50 cm) tall and can weigh more than 550 lb (250 kg). That's impressive considering that when they are born they weigh just 1.2–2.6 oz (50–75 g) and can fit on your hand. Goliath, a tortoise from Santa Cruz, grew even bigger. He was 4.5 ft (1.36 m) long, 2.25 ft (68.5 cm) tall and he weighed a whopping 919 lb (417 kg)!

How many are found on the islands?

Around 20,000 of these creatures are found in the Galápagos today, but the numbers were quite different in the past. Before humans arrived, there may have been more than 100,000 giant tortoises on the Islands. Tens of thousands were killed by sailors for food, and by the 1970s there were only around 3000 left. Since that time, breeding programs have helped increase numbers.

giant tortoise on San Cristobal Island

What do they eat?

Galápagos tortoises are plant-eaters. They mostly feed on cactuses, grasses, leaves, and fruit. Young tortoises are particularly greedy and can eat about a sixth of their body weight in food every day! In hard times, tortoises can go without food or water for many months.

Are there different types of Galápagos giant tortoise?

Yes! Tortoises that grow up on one island have differences compared to those from other islands. They may vary in size or the shape of their top shell, which is called a carapace. Some islands' tortoises have a dome-shaped carapace, while others have a carapace shaped like a saddle.

The **GALAPAGOS SHARK** hunts bony fish, sea lions, and marine iguanas, which it attacks using its 14 rows of sharp teeth. Baby sharks stay in shallow waters for fear of adults of their own species turning cannibal and eating them!

UNDERWATER LIFE

More than 400 types of fish and many other marine creatures, including the Pacific seahorse and various sharks, are found in the waters around the Galápagos. Here are some of the most fascinating!

One visitor to the coastal waters of the islands is the giant **OCEAN SUNFISH**. It's the biggest bony fish in the world. Growing large on its diet of jellyfish and crustaceans, such as shrimp, this fish can measure up to 13.8 ft (4.2 m) by 10 ft (3 m) and weigh more than 4850 lb (2200 kg). That's heavier than three cows!

Growing up to 13 in (35 cm) long, **KING ANGELFISH** are brightly colored tropical fish that eat sponges and plankton but also nibble parasites off fearsome hammerhead sharks!

GALAPAGOS CLINGFISH are well named. These strange fish have a large sucker on their underside, which they use to attach themselves firmly to rocks so they can feed without the waves and tides washing them away.

Adult **GALAPAGOS GREEN TURTLES** lay ping-pong-ball-sized eggs on the shore but spend the rest of their time at sea. They are mostly vegetarian, but young turtles will eat what they can, including jellyfish.

Many patterned fish inhabit the waters around the islands, including the **ZEBRA MORAY**, a strikingly striped fish that lives close to the seafloor, where it can grow up to 5 ft (1.5 m) long.

TOP 10

UNUSUAL INHABITANTS

Check out these awesome—
and very strange—animals!

1 Red-lipped batfish

With its bright-red, puffy lips, this fish looks
as strange as its name. What's more, it is a
terrible swimmer and prefers to walk along
the ocean floor using its fins as feet!

2. Magnificent frigatebird

These birds steal food from others in midair. The males inflate a throat pouch to impress females.

7. Scalloped hammerhead

This strange shark can see behind and above itself but cannot view what's right in front of its nose!

3. Fiddler crab

Fiddler crabs change color, turning dark in the day and lighter at night. Males have one huge claw to impress females.

8. Trumpetfish

These super-slim fish can change color to look like the fish they are hunting. That's sneaky!

4. Pink iguana

The pink iguana was only confirmed as a new species in 2009. It is found on Isabela Island and nowhere else.

9. Lava lizard

This lively lizard guards its territory fiercely. It performs a series of press-ups to show off its strength and warn off predators.

5. Galápagos mockingbird

Curious and fearless, these birds can fly, but they sometimes choose to run after prey instead.

10. Concentric puffer

This fish protects itself from predators by puffing up its body so that it looks too big to attack.

6. Pacific seahorse

The female of this striking creature produces the eggs, then puts them in a pouch in the male's body to keep safe until they hatch.

Which unusual inhabitant is your number one?

BLUE-FOOTED BOOBIES

Named after the Spanish word for "foolish," this comical-looking bird is a firm favorite of tourists. The blue-footed booby appears slightly clumsy on land as it waddles around on its bright-blue feet. At sea and in the air, though, it is masterful. The bird folds back its wings as it dives steeply and plunges into the sea at speeds of over 55 mph (90 kph).

Fabulous feet

Boobies appear very proud of their bright-blue feet. Males perform complicated and goofy dances to impress females in the breeding season. Their feet are also used to cover young chicks to keep them safe and warm. Younger, healthier birds tend to have brighter feet.

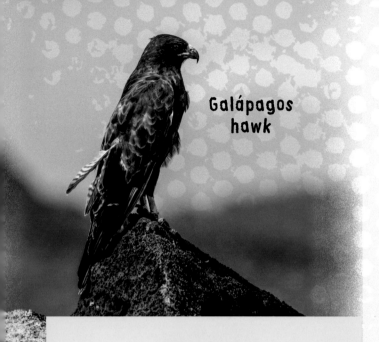

Galápagos
hawk

ISLAND

Galápagos creatures grab their dinner in many ways, as these amazing hunters prove.

VAMPIRE FINCH

The vampire finch weighs just 0.5 oz (15 g), but when insects and seeds are scarce, it pecks at larger birds to drink their warm blood. It will also smash other birds' eggs by rolling them downhill, using its feet to make the eggs crash into rocks.

blood sucker!

VERMILION FLYCATCHER

This bright-red bird stands out not just visually, but because of its outstanding reactions in the air. With very sharp eyesight, it can catch whizzing flies, beetles, and bees. The flycatcher can also hover in midair and swoop down on insects perched on the ground.

take aim

HUNTERS

GALAPAGOS RACER

One of the islands' few land snakes has developed a taste for fish . . . so it goes fishing! The racer will slither along coastlines and hang over the edge of rock pools before lunging to pluck small fish out of the water with devastating accuracy.

frightening fishing

GALAPAGOS GIANT CENTIPEDE

Most centipedes are 0.4–0.8 in (1–2 cm) long, but this centipede grows as long as a large ruler: 12 in (30 cm)! It hides in large cracks and crevices waiting for prey, such as large insects, lizards, and even rats, which it grips with its 46 legs and injects with a deadly venom.

lots of legs

SHIP AHOY!

ISLAND FACTS

1535

In 1535, the Bishop of Panama, Tomás de Berlanga, was sailing close to the coast of South America, heading for Peru, when the winds calmed and the ocean currents started carrying his ship westwards out into the Pacific Ocean. The ship became the first ever to reach the Galápagos. The bishop was not impressed by the islands and described the birds there as: "So silly, they know not how to fly."

1600s

The Galápagos Islands were added to maps in the late 16th century. In the following century, they were used as a hideout by pirates.

1784–1860

From the 1780s, the islands were used as a base for whaling ships. **Whalers** hunted sperm whales for their oil; they also captured Galápagos fur seals for their skin and giant tortoises for their meat. Between 1784 and 1860, whalers took more than 100,000 tortoises from the islands. Herman Melville, a sailor on a whaling ship, wrote a famous novel about a whale, called *Moby Dick*.

picture from "Moby Dick"

Until the building of airports on the islands, every human visitor arrived by boat. Find out which vessels sailed the Pacific Ocean to reach the Galápagos.

1807

No one lived on the island until the eccentric adventurer Patrick Watkins settled on Floreana Island in 1807 for several years. He used to kidnap sailors from passing ships and get them to work for him, and once he even stole a ship to sail to Ecuador!

1939–45

US forces sent ships and planes to the Galápagos during World War II. They built a base and airstrip on Baltra Island to guard against enemy submarines. The airstrip later became Seymour Airport.

2011

In 2011, an extraordinary boat reached Santa Cruz Island. The 100-ft- (31-m-) long *PlanetSolar Tûranor* isn't powered by wind or diesel engines, but by solar panels, which turn sunlight into electricity. It's the world largest solar boat and docked at the Galápagos on its way across the Pacific on a round-the-world journey.

TODAY

Today, the Galápagos welcome dozens of boats and ships. Small cruise liners and large yachts allow people to live on board but explore the islands during the day.

PlanetSolar Tûranor

PIRATES!

In the time between the islands being discovered in the 16th century and people settling there permanently, the Galápagos had a wild history, as a place where pirates moored, met, and battled.

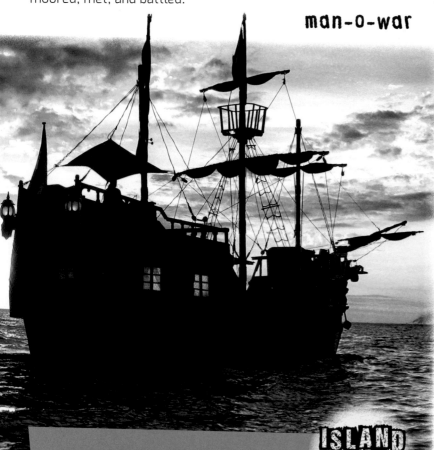

man-o-war

By the **17TH CENTURY**, Spain controlled much of South and Central America. Spanish ships ferried gold and other riches back from these regions to Europe. These ships were often targets for ruthless pirates sailing the Pacific for treasure ships to loot, such as Dutchman Jacob L'Hermite Clerk and British pirates John Cook, Richard Hawkins, and Henry Morgan.

PIRATE SHIPS used the Galápagos as a place to escape to after their raids. They were far enough from the South American coast to avoid being chased, but close enough to the main **shipping routes** to launch new raids. No one knows if they ever buried any of their captured treasure on the islands.

Henry Morgan

pirate map

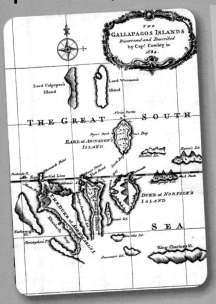

ISLAND FACT

In 1684, the *Bachelor's Delight* pirate ship landed on Santiago Island in a bay now called **BUCCANEER'S COVE**. A member of its crew, Ambrose Cowley, made one of the first detailed maps of the island. He named islands and features after English kings or nobles. These were later changed to Spanish names.

pieces of eight

ISLAND FACT

The first visit to the Galápagos by **BRITISH PIRATE** and naturalist William Dampier was in the 1680s, on a ship stolen by pirates. He returned to the islands during a voyage in which he captured a Spanish ship packed with gold. He wrote a best-selling book about his travels, *A New Voyage Round the World*.

Shiver me timbers!

ISLAND FACT

By 1800, the classic age of piracy was over, but battling didn't stop. An American ship captain, David Porter, hunted down British whaling ships close to the Galápagos in his warship, The *Essex*. In 1813, he attacked and either captured or destroyed four British vessels.

Charles Darwin

DARWIN'S VOYAGE OF DISCOVERY

Find out how Charles Darwin used the Galápagos as inspiration for his groundbreaking theories.

In **DECEMBER 1831**, this 22-year-old naturalist boarded a sailing ship, HMS *Beagle*, at the start of a five-year-long, round-the-world voyage. Along the way, Charles Darwin visited the Galápagos, which would inspire his theories that changed how people looked at the natural world.

HMS *BEAGLE* was captained by Robert Fitzroy on a long voyage making maps and surveys of the sea and coastlines of South America.

Darwin kept daily records of every creature and plant he saw at sea or on land when the ship moored. Darwin also collected **FOSSILS**. He saw how some of these fossils were similar to living species and wondered how new species developed.

IN SEPTEMBER 1835, the *Beagle* reached the Galápagos, stopping first at San Cristóbal Island, before later traveling to Floreana, Isabela, and

"The misery I endured from **SEASICKNESS** is beyond what I ever guessed at."—Charles Darwin on his voyage on HMS *Beagle*.

Santiago islands. Darwin was amazed by the giant tortoises, and in five weeks on the islands collected many samples of plants, birds, and animals. He noticed that the wildlife on each island differed and had adapted to suit its environment.

DARWIN RETURNED home on the *Beagle* in 1836, full of questions about what he had seen. Over the next 25 years, he worked on his theories and published his book, *On the Origin of Species*, in 1859. In it, he explained how all species of living things developed or evolved from earlier lifeforms. For example, birds evolved from reptiles, while humans and apes evolved from the same common ancestor.

Darwin and the crew of the *Beagle* ate iguanas and giant tortoises taken from the islands. They also kept two of the **TORTOISES** as pets.

Darwin later explained how species changed by a process he called **NATURAL SELECTION**.

ON THE COAST

More than 80 percent of the Galápagos' 25,000 inhabitants live in four towns or villages, all of which lie on the coast. Most people or their ancestors have come from Ecuador to settle. Around 6000 people live in the capital, Puerto Baquerizo Moreno, on San Cristóbal Island. Puerto Ayora on Santa Cruz, though, is bigger with over 9200 inhabitants.

Baltra Island stall

FOOD AND WATER

The people who live on the islands know fresh water is rare and precious; most households collect and store rainwater. While some crops, such as plantain and coffee—the Galápagos' main export—are grown locally, most food is brought in by ship. More than 1100 crates of supplies arrive in ships at Puerto Ayora every day!

San Cristobal dock

ISLANDS

Learn about the people (known as Galápagueños) who call the Galápagos Islands home.

PEOPLE AT WORK

Some people farm, fish, or provide services for the local community, such as nurses, teachers, and shopkeepers. Most are involved in the tourism industry, working in national parks, hotels, piloting water taxis, or as guides, teaching visitors about the islands. More than 200,000 tourists visit the Galápagos each year.

Santa Cruz tour boats

PLAY TIME

Soccer is particularly popular on the islands. In 2015, Galápagueños celebrated their first player to make it to a FIFA World Cup—female soccer star Denise Andrea Pesántes.

Floreana Island soccer players

CLOSE UP

GALAPAGOS DAY

This local woman, dressed in bright, traditional clothes, dances in a parade along the streets of Galápagos' biggest town, Puerto Ayora. She is part of the celebrations for Galápagos Day, a national holiday on the islands every year on February 12—the day that the islands are celebrated for becoming a territory of Ecuador. It also happens to be the date of the birthday of its most famous visitor: Charles Darwin.

Early settlers

For many years, the Galápagos were under Spain's control, until 1832 when a general from Ecuador sent 12 men to set up a small **colony** on Floreana Island. More settlers came and went, and the islands were used as prisons before larger villages and towns were built. The human population of the Galápagos has risen from just 1300 people in 1950 to over 26,000 today.

LIVING WITH NATURE

The natural world of the Galápagos is extraordinary but fragile. To protect the hundreds of rare plants and animal species and their habitats, the government of Ecuador created the Galápagos National Park in 1959. The park covers 97 percent of the Galápagos' territory. Only four of the islands have permanent places for people to live.

ISLAND FACT

The islands are left mainly unspoiled and certain parts can be visited only with an official guide. In 1986, a large area of sea surrounding the islands was turned into a marine reserve. However, humans still have a negative impact on the environment through transportation and pollution.

beach
buddies

caution: tortoise crossing

LOCAL PEOPLE have learned to live with the natural wonders around them and depend on them to attract tourists to the islands. A car may have to stop on a road or track to let a giant tortoise slowly cross, while benches in the towns are often occupied by sea lions taking a nap!

free fish food

The Santa Cruz **FISH MARKET** in Puerto Ayora is often overrun with sea lions, frigatebirds, and pelicans on the lookout for a meal. Such creatures will sometimes lurk close to fishing boats as well, hoping to steal some of the fish in the catch.

camera curious

Visitors shouldn't get too close to the animals, but many creatures on the **GALAPAGOS** are not afraid of humans. Hood mockingbirds are so fearless that they sometimes dip their beak into people's drinks to take a sip!

WHALE SHARK CONSERVATION

Magnificent whale sharks are frequent visitors to the Galápagos Marine Reserve, mostly between June and November. These huge creatures can measure 39 ft (12 m) long and weigh as much as 20 tons. Pregnant females can carry over 300 babies inside their body. In 2011, to learn more about these mysterious creatures, scientists tagged some to discover their migration routes between Ecuador, Peru, and the Galápagos.

More about whale sharks

Whale sharks have an enormous mouth—
up to 4.5 ft (1.4 m) wide—almost as wide as you
are tall! But relax, they don't feed on people
or any large sea life. Instead, they use their
mouth as a giant sieve to gather and filter large
amounts of tiny plankton to feed on.

TOP 10 LANDMARKS

Check out some of the fascinating landmarks around the islands.

1 Lighthouse

A lighthouse stands above Mann Beach near Puerto Baquerizo Moreno warning ships about rocks out at sea.

2 Post Office Bay

In 1793, a barrel was placed on Floreana Island so whalers could post their letters; sailors who were going home would deliver them for free.

7 Pinnacle Rock

Bartolomé Island's Pinnacle Rock is a great snorkeling spot. You can swim with penguins, turtles, and even white-tipped sharks!

3 Shipwreck!

A German World War I ship, *The Caragua*, sank out at sea near Mann Beach. It is now a habitat for fish, sea lions, and sea turtles.

8 Wall of Tears

This stone wall on Isabela Island was built by prisoners in 1945–59. In 1958, 21 prisoners escaped the islands in a stolen yacht.

4 Iglesia Cristo Salvador

This church on Isabela Island features painted scenes of local creatures, such as penguins.

9 Artful arch

At Puerto Ayora, you'll find an arch decorated with Galápagos creatures, such as iguanas, giant tortoises, and blue-footed boobies.

5 Great stone head

This stone head on Floreana Island tricked archaeologists into thinking it was carved by ancient peoples. It was just a practical joke—it was carved in the 1930s!

10 Research station

The Charles Darwin Research Station on Santa Cruz is home to over 200 scientists. Their work includes hand rearing Galápagos tortoises.

6 Darwin's Arch

You can visit many sites named after Charles Darwin, including this archway, which is just off Darwin Island.

Which landmark would you like to visit?

ALL ABOUT CONSERVATION

Find answers to your questions about conservation on the Galápagos.

What rules do visitors have to follow?

Visitors to the Galápagos must not bring in any plants or animals, which could disrupt life on the island, so people and their bags are checked thoroughly for seeds, insects, and other life. Fires, littering, and flash photography are banned to avoid disturbing the animals, and visitors can only travel to many sites with official guides. The aim is to preserve these incredible islands for future generations of plants, wildlife, and human visitors.

What threats do Galápagos wildlife?

Many! Growing numbers of human residents and visitors mean sewage, garbage, and other waste pollute the land and water. Shipping accidents can be deadly: An oil spill from a tanker ship in 2001 killed more than 15,000 iguanas on Santa Fé. Overfishing the sea surrounding the islands deprives some marine creatures of food. Plus climate change threatens the delicate balance of life on the islands.

How can conservation help?

Conservationists have tried to tackle some invasive species, such as goats, by removing them from some of the islands. People are encouraged to produce less waste and to use renewable energies, such as solar power, which cause less pollution. Some people have set up breeding programs, protecting eggs and young birds and animals until they are ready to be released into the wild.

Are any creatures endangered?

Yes. According to the Galápagos Conservation Trust, over 50 species are critically endangered. These include two species of giant tortoise, the pink lava lizard, and some species of bird, such as the mangrove finch and waved albatross. In the 20th century, a number of Galápagos species died out, including a species of flycatcher bird and Darwin's Galápagos mouse.

THE GREAT GALÁPAGOS Quiz

So you think you're a Galápagos genius? Test your knowledge by completing this quiz! When you've answered all of the questions, turn to page 63 to check your score.

 Which is the nearest country to the Galápagos?
a) Brazil
b) Colombia
c) Ecuador

 In which ocean would you find the islands?
a) Atlantic
b) Indian
c) Pacific

 What fish can change its appearance to look like the animal it is hunting?
a) Flutefish
b) Saxaphonefish
c) Trumpetfish

 On which island would you find the Galápagos' highest peak, Wolf Volcano?
a) Darwin
b) Isabela
c) Santa Cruz

 Which Galápagos creature performs press-ups to warn other creatures away from its territory?
a) Galápagos sea lion
b) Hoary bat
c) Lava lizard

 Which famous scientist visited the Galápagos in the 1830s and formed theories on how living things evolve?
a) Albert Einstein
b) Charles Darwin
c) Stephen Hawking

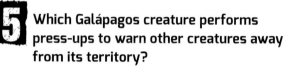 **Which bird has a bright-red throat pouch and steals food from other birds in midair?**
a) Galápagos hawk
b) Lava heron
c) Magnificent frigatebird

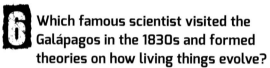 **Which is the biggest crop grown in the Galápagos to be sold overseas?**
a) Coffee
b) Cotton
c) Mangoes

 Which type of bird sometimes rests on the head of a brown pelican and tries to steal fish from it?
a) Brown noddy
b) Galápagos hawk
c) Red-footed booby

 Which Galápagos island was Lonesome George from?
a) Pinta
b) Rábida
c) Santa Cruz

 What sort of creature is the fish-eating Galápagos racer?
a) A seabird
b) A seal
c) A snake

 How many rows of sharp teeth does a Galápagos shark's mouth contain?
a) 3
b) 14
c) 32

 On which island would you find the Wall of Tears?
a) Floreana Island
b) Isabela Island
c) Santiago Island

 Which date is celebrated as Galápagos Day each year?
a) February 12
b) April 5
c) June 10

 On which island would you find the flushing water pool called Darwin's Toilet?
a) Española
b) Floreana
c) Santiago

 What was the name of the ship that carried Charles Darwin to the Galápagos in the 1830s?
a) HMS *Beagle*
b) HMS *Intrepid*
c) *PlanetSolar Turanor*

 Which is the biggest town in the Galápagos?
a) Puerto Ayora
b) Puerto Baquerizo Moreno
c) Puerto Villamil

 What is the name of the Galápagos' largest freshwater lake found on San Cristóbal Island?
a) Devil's Crown
b) El Junco
c) La Cumbre

GLOSSARY

archipelago
A group or chain of, usually small, islands, such as the Galápagos Islands.

breeding
When pairs of creatures mate to reproduce new members of their species.

canyon
A deep, usually narrow, valley with steep sides.

climate
The weather conditions usually found in an area of the planet over a period of time.

cold-blooded
Creatures whose blood and body temperature varies depending on their environment. Many creatures including fish, snakes, and lizards are cold-blooded.

colony
A group of creatures, such as birds, that all live in the same area.

coral
Tiny, soft-bodied sea creatures, whose hard outer skeletons form coral reefs.

endemic
A species of living thing that is found in only one place or area. Many of the Galápagos Islands' species of plants and creatures are endemic.

environment
The surroundings that a creature or plant lives in.

plankton
Tiny, shrimplike creatures, which live in huge numbers in seas and oceans.

shipping route
A path through the sea which is used regularly by ships as they sail from place to place.

tectonic plates
The massive plates which make up Earth's rocky crust.

tide
The rising and falling of the sea every day, caused by the attraction of the Sun and Moon with Earth.

vegetarian
A person or creature that does not eat any meat or fish.

whalers
People who use boats and ships to kill and capture whales in order to sell them for their meat, oil, or fatty blubber.

fossils
The remains or impression of a prehistoric living thing which is preserved in rock.

freshwater
Naturally-occurring water in rivers, streams, lakes, and ice caps that is not saltwater (water found in the seas and oceans).

hot spot
An area below Earth's surface, usually in a region of volcanic activity, which is hotter than the surrounding regions.

islet
A small island.

lava
Hot, molten rock which has reached Earth's surface, often from a volcano erupting.

magma
Hot, runny rock found just below the surface of Earth.

naturalist
A person who studies the plants and creatures found on Earth.

QUIZ ANSWERS: 1 = c, 2 = c, 3 = c, 4 = b, 5 = c, 6 = b, 7 = c, 8 = a, 9 = a, 10 = A, 11 = c, 12 = b, 13 = b, 14 = a, 15 = c, 16 = a, 17 = a, 18 = b.

INDEX

A
acacia trees 15
albatrosses 27, 59
angelfish 33
archipelago 6
arid zone 15

B
Bainbridge Rocks 10, 19
Bartolomé Island 10, 19
batfish 34
bird life 14, 17, 19, 22, 23, 26–27, 35, 36–37, 38, 53, 59
boobies 27, 36–37
brown noddies 27

C
cactuses 15, 16–17
calderas 13
canyons 18
caves 19
centipedes 39
climate 11
clingfish 33
coastal zone 14
conservation 58–59
coral reefs 19
cormorants 23
crabs 24–25, 35
Cracks, The 18

D, E
Darwin, Charles 28, 46–47, 50, 57
Darwin's Toilet 19
Devil's Crown 19
doves 14, 27
Ecuador 6, 48, 50, 51
employment 49
endangered species 59
endemic species 22, 23
environment, threats to 52, 58, 59
Equator 10
Española Island 10, 19
evolution 47

F
farming 48
Fernandina Island 10, 19
finches 14, 17, 27, 38, 59
fish 32–33, 34, 35, 57
Floreana Island 10, 19, 41, 57
flycatchers 38
frigatebirds 14, 35, 53
fur seals 22, 42

G, H
Galápagos Day 50
Galápagos Marine Reserve 52, 54, 55
Galápagos National Park 52
Galápagueños 48–51
Genovesa Island 10, 28
hawks 22, 27
herons 27
hot spots 11
humid zone 14

I, L
iguanas 15, 17, 19, 25, 28–29, 35, 47, 59
Isabela Island 10, 13, 19, 27, 28, 57
islands and islets 10, 18–19
landmarks 56–57
lava 12, 18, 19
lava cactuses 15
lava lizards 15, 22, 35, 59
lava tubes 12
locusts 22

M, O
mangrove trees 14
marine life 32–33, 34, 35, 54–55, 57, 59
mockingbirds 35, 53
ocean currents 11

P
Pacific Ocean 6, 10, 12
pelicans 14, 26, 53
penguins 27, 57
Pinnacle Rock 57
Pinta Island 10, 22
pirates 42, 44–45
plants 14, 15, 16–17
population 48–51
prickly pears 16–17
Puerto Ayora 10, 48, 50, 57
Puerto Baquerizo Moreno 10, 48
pufferfish 35

R, S, T
Rábida Island 10, 19
San Cristóbal Island 10, 19, 46, 48
Santa Cruz Island 10, 18, 30, 48
Santiago Island 19, 45
scalesia trees 14
sea lions 23, 53
seahorses 35
sharks 19, 32, 33, 35, 54–55, 57
ships and boats 42–43, 44, 45, 46, 47, 59
snakes 39
sunfish 33
tectonic plates 10, 11
tortoises 6, 14, 17, 22, 30–31, 42, 47, 53, 57, 59
tourism 49, 58
tropicbirds 27
trumpetfish 35
turtles 33, 57

V, W, Z
volcanoes 11, 12–13, 19
Wall of Tears 57
whale sharks 54–55
whaling 42, 45
wildlife 14, 15, 17, 19, 22–39, 47, 52–55, 57, 59
Wolf Volcano 13, 19
zebra moray 33